Splat!

WITHDRAWN

Eric Walters

Orca Currents

ORCA BOOK PUBLISHERS

Library and Archives Canada Cataloguing in Publication
Walters, Eric, 1957-

Splat! / written by Eric Walters.

(Orca currents)

ISBN 978-1-55143-988-4 (bound)--ISBN 978-1-55143-986-0 (pbk.)

I. Title. II. Series.
PS8595.A598S63   2008 jC813'.54   C2007-906965-7

Summary: Keegan and Alex decide to add some excitement to the
town's tomato festival.

First published in the United States, 2008
Library of Congress Control Number: 2007940948

Orca Book Publishers gratefully acknowledges the support for its publishing
programs provided by the following agencies: the Government of Canada
through the Book Publishing Industry Development Program and the
Canada Council for the Arts, and the Province of British Columbia
through the BC Arts Council and the Book Publishing Tax Credit.

Cover design by Teresa Bubela
Cover photography by Corbis

Orca Book Publishers
PO Box 5626, Station B
Victoria, BC Canada
V8R 6S4

Orca Book Publishers
PO Box 468
Custer, WA USA
98240-0468

www.orcabook.com
Printed and bound in Canada.
Printed on 100% recycled paper.
11 10 09 • 4 3 2

chapter one

The police car turned down the lane and crept along the dirt road toward us.

I nudged Keegan.

"Yeah, I see it," he said.

Keegan turned away to stare out at the lake. I watched the car out of the corner of my eye. I didn't want the cops to know that I'd even seen them. The car came to a stop on the other side of the fence, across the stretch of beach from where we sat on the picnic bench.

"Could you see who's in the car?" he asked.

"Couldn't tell."

We knew every cop in town. Just like every cop knew us.

"What do you think they're doing?" I asked.

"Probably just looking for a place to have a donut and catch up on their sleep."

"I hope that's all that they want," I said.

"Alex, you sound guilty."

"I'm *not* guilty. Besides, we really aren't doing anything wrong."

"The day is young," Keegan said.

He turned slightly and gave me that smirky smile of his—the one he often flashed before we started to do something we shouldn't.

There was a honking of a car horn, and I almost spun around to look, but didn't.

"Ignore him," Keegan said. "He probably isn't aiming that at us anyway."

"Who do *you* think he's honking at?"

"Don't know. Don't care. If he wants us he'll have to do more than just tap on his—"

The siren of the car screamed for a few seconds, cutting off the end of Keegan's sentence.

"Well?" I asked.

"Probably wants somebody else."

"There's only us and them," I said, gesturing toward a woman and her two little kids, wading in the water. The rest of the beach was deserted. It was overcast, and it had been raining or there would have been a lot more people.

"You know, she does look a bit suspicious," Keegan said.

"The woman with the kids?"

"You think she kidnapped those children?"

I chuckled. "I guess there's a possibility," I admitted. "Not big, but a statistical possibility."

"And if anybody knows the statistics it would be you."

I had this strange ability to memorize

statistics and play with numbers—especially when those numbers involved money.

"Keegan and Alex!" the PA system of the police car blared out.

I recognized the voice. It was Clyde.

Keegan looked over at me. "I guess they *do* want us."

He went to stand up, and I put my hand on his shoulder to hold him in place.

"Maybe those *kids* are named Keegan and Alex," I said, pointing down the beach at the toddlers, "and the police want them and not their mother."

Keegan burst into laughter and sat down again.

"I know you can hear me!" Clyde's amplified voice called out. "Get off that picnic table and come here, *now*!"

Keegan looked over at me. He pointed at the table, then at himself and then at me. I knew what he meant—picnic table, Keegan, Alex—we fit all the pieces.

"What would happen if we just kept ignoring him?" Keegan asked.

"They'd probably come over and get us," I said. "But they wouldn't be happy."

"How about if we ran?" he questioned.

"Even less happy when they did catch us," I said.

"They couldn't catch us. Clyde would be out of breath just walking over here, so forget the running part. We could out-*walk* the two of them easy."

"But since they know where we hang out, go to school and live, I think that even the two of them would eventually catch us."

"Good point," said Keegan.

"Aren't you at least a little bit curious to know want they want?" I asked.

"Curiosity killed the cat."

We heard the car's doors slam. They'd gotten out of the car.

"Okay, we'll go over," he said.

Keegan stood up and raised his hands over his head—his skateboard in one hand. I did the same thing.

"Don't shoot!" he yelled. "We are not armed!"

With our arms above our heads we slowly walked over. I couldn't believe how heavy my skateboard was when I held it above my head. I wished we could put our hands down as we walked across the strip of beach.

"What exactly are you two doing?" Clyde asked.

Beside him was his partner, Bernie. Everybody—including all the other cops—called them Bonnie and Clyde like the old-time gangsters. They weren't amused by that. Everybody else was very amused.

"We didn't want to risk you taking a shot at us for resisting arrest," Keegan said.

"Believe me, I'd like to give both of you a shot—a swift kick in the butt."

"Sounds like police brutality," Keegan suggested. "What would the chief of police think about that?"

"He'd probably give us a raise *and* a promotion. Get in the car."

"We weren't doing anything wrong," I said.

"Chief wants to see both of you right

away, so I figure you *were* doing something wrong."

"Did he say what?" I asked.

"You sound guilty," Clyde said.

"He's right," Keegan agreed. "You *do* sound guilty. Didn't I just tell you that? What exactly did you do?"

"I didn't do anything!" I exclaimed. "I was with you all day!"

Keegan turned to Bernie. "I want you to know that *I* didn't do anything, and I'm not going to be an alibi witness for him. Whatever he did, I know nothing about it, and if I did, I'd rat him out in a second. Maybe you could throw him into the interview room and browbeat a confession out of him. You could break this whole thing wide open and—"

"Get in," Bernie said as he opened the back passenger door.

"Now," Clyde said, pointing. "No more discussion."

I climbed in, and Keegan followed. Bernie slammed the door closed, locking us in. I hated the back of police cars—no handles, no way out until they let you out. Sort of like little rolling jails.

"I've got to stop hanging around with you," Keegan said. "You're obviously a bad influence."

"He's a bad influence?" Clyde said. He and Bernie began laughing.

Clyde started the car.

"Really, do either of you know what this is about?" Keegan asked.

"He didn't give us reasons, he just gave us orders," Bernie said.

"That's right. Pick them up and bring them both over to the mayor's office."

"The mayor wants to see us?" Keegan asked, looking over at me for an explanation.

"The mayor *and* the chief," Clyde said. "Whatever you two did I think you're going to regret doing it."

I didn't know what it was, but I already did regret it.

"Maybe we should have made a run for it," I said under my breath.

chapter two

Bonnie and Clyde dropped us off at city hall. We waved as they drove away.

"So, do we go up to the mayor's office?" Keegan asked.

"Do you know how much trouble we'd be in if we didn't?"

"How much?"

"Let's not find out. Besides, we didn't do anything wrong," I reasoned.

"If we didn't, why do you think they put out an all-points bulletin for us?"

"This is Leamington. What's the worst thing that has ever happened around here? Some overturned garbage cans, a missing cat?"

"Only thing I can think of is somebody complained we were skateboarding on private property," Keegan said.

"That wouldn't be a problem if they'd build us a halfway decent skate park."

"You're right about that," said Keegan. "We must have the most pathetic park in the entire world. It's embarrassing."

"So, come on, let's go upstairs and find out. It's not like we're on *America's Most Wanted* or anything. Don't be afraid," I said. "Do you want to hold my hand?"

"Okay, fine, let's go."

We went up the stairs. The outer office was empty except for the secretary, Mrs. Wallace. She was sitting at her desk pretending to be working but actually watching the TV on in the corner. She didn't look up as we entered.

"Hello," I said when I reached her desk. "How are you?"

She looked up and smiled. "I'm doing just fine. So nice of you to ask."

She was always kind to me, but then again, what choice did she have?

"That's *nice* to hear," Keegan said. "Do you have any idea what this is all about?" Keegan asked.

"Yes, I do know," she said, going back to pretending to work.

"Are you going to tell us?" Keegan pressed.

"No."

She worked—watching the TV with the sound off—but I saw a small smile creep onto her face. She didn't like Keegan at all.

That TV was always on, but the sound was always off. Mrs. Wallace must have been able to read lips or something.

"Do you think we're going to be waiting long?" Keegan asked.

He was, as always, persistent.

"You'll be waiting as long as it takes," she said, shooting Keegan an evil eye.

She then turned to me and smiled.

"So, Alex, how is that wonderful sister of yours?"

"She's still pretty *wonderful*," I answered, trying to hide the sarcasm in my voice.

"I'm sure she's settled in and doing well," she said.

"My guess is that she's doing wonderful," I said.

"Yes, wonderful," Keegan agreed.

My sister had just started first year university—on a scholarship—and had moved out of town.

"I've always predicted that girl would go far."

"Clear across the country," I said.

"Pardon?"

"Her university is on the other side of the country...you know...she went far."

"Oh, you were telling *a joke*," she said and sort of laughed—a pity laugh.

"Got to work on those jokes," Keegan said under his breath so only I could hear him.

"I meant she'll go far in whatever field she pursues. She is so dedicated, so committed, so smart."

I could have added so boring and so annoying, but I just smiled and nodded.

"So, what are you watching?" Keegan asked her.

"I'm not watching anything," she said. "That TV is for people waiting to see the mayor."

"In that case could we turn up the sound and change to something other than a soap opera?"

Before she could answer, the door opened and out walked a bunch of men—the most important business leaders in the whole town! What did all of them have to do with us? This couldn't be a good sign.

I looked over at Keegan. He looked as worried as I felt.

These guys were all the movers and shakers of our town...although you didn't have to do much moving or shaking to make it big here. They were all so busy talking and laughing and slapping each other on the back that they didn't seem to notice us at first.

Then, one by one, some of them said

hello to us or nodded a greeting. They all knew us. That was one of the things about Leamington. Everybody knew everybody else. When I was little I liked that. Now it was just boring and annoying.

Slowly they all finished saying their goodbyes and left, until the room was empty except for me and Keegan, and the chief, mayor and his secretary.

"In," the chief said, pointing toward the mayor's office.

He was a man of few words. Maybe when you carried a gun you didn't need to say much. I certainly wasn't going to argue with him.

We shuffled in and sat down.

"Do you two know why you're here?" the chief asked.

"I was hoping you'd know," Keegan said.

The chief looked like he was thinking of using his gun.

"Whatever it is we didn't do it, or mean to do it, and we won't do it again," I said before any gunplay could happen.

"That pretty well covers all the bases," the chief said. "You're sounding guilty."

"That's what everybody is saying," Keegan agreed.

"Well, hanging around with you can certainly lead to being guilty of something," the chief said. "But you're not here because you did anything wrong...at least that I know of."

"Then why are we here?" I asked.

"The Tomato Festival," he said.

Then it all started to make sense. Those people who had been in the office in that meeting were all the people who would most likely be working on the Tomato Festival.

"You know how important the festival is," the mayor said.

I was tempted to say something about how stupid it was, but I knew better. People here, especially if you were the mayor or the police chief or a businessman, took the Tomato Festival very seriously. Leamington was the tomato capital of the country. Almost everything around here revolved around growing, canning or shipping tomatoes. And every year there was a big festival in town to celebrate tomatoes.

"But what has any of that got to do with us in general, and specifically, us being here now?" Keegan asked.

"Almost every young person in town is involved in the festival in one way or another," the chief said.

"None of our friends," Keegan said.

"Not a one," I agreed.

"That maybe says something about your choice in friends," the chief said.

Were we here to get a lecture about our choice of friends? I knew that some of them were a little questionable. Whenever this subject came up I always mentioned David and Sam. They were our friends, but they were also honor students, polite and family friends. They were above objection.

"And you two are *going* to become involved," the chief said. "Consider yourselves officially *volunteered*."

"You can't be volunteered!" Keegan protested. "It doesn't work like that."

"He's right," I agreed. "That isn't even good grammar."

"I just don't know why this is such a problem for you boys. Alex, you used to love the festival."

"I also used to be six, not almost sixteen."

"I'm a lot older than sixteen and I still love the festival," the mayor said. "Everybody loves the festival, right?" he asked the chief. "Everybody I know. I know for a fact that *your* sister still loves the festival," he said, pointing at me.

I hated comparisons to her. "And just what is my sister doing at this year's festival?" I asked.

"She *would* be doing something if she wasn't at university."

And if she hadn't chosen a university so far away that she would have dropped into the Pacific if she went any farther. Didn't anybody except me know that escaping the Tomato Festival was part of the reason she choose a school so far away?

"I just want you to follow in her footsteps," the mayor said.

"Wasn't she Miss Tomato Festival two years ago?" Keegan asked. "I'm not sure, but I don't think Alex could follow those specific footsteps," Keegan said.

"Keegan!" the chief warned him.

"I'm just having a hard time picturing Alex in a dress and heels."

"That you'd even *try* to picture me that way is disturbing," I said.

"But strangely compelling in a surreal way," Keegan added.

"Both of you stop now!" the mayor said. "Do you two always have to behave like you have an unspoken contest to see who can be the most ridiculous?"

Keegan and I exchanged a look. Actually it was a spoken, agreed-to contest. So far today Keegan was winning, but the day was still early.

"That's the problem with you two," the chief said. "Instead of one of you being reasonable when the other suggests something stupid you just egg each other on."

"And I wouldn't know anybody like that," I said.

Keegan chuckled, and both men looked sheepish.

I knew they'd been friends since they were little and I'd heard stories about things the two of them had gotten into. In a small town it was pretty hard to escape your past.

"Just because we made some mistakes doesn't mean you two have to make the same mistakes," the chief said.

"Are you suggesting that we make new mistakes?" I asked.

The mayor got all red in the face—actually *more* red in the face. He and I had the same red hair and freckles.

Time to change the subject.

"Why is it so important for us to be involved?" I asked, trying to reason our way out of this.

"Every person on the whole committee has at least one child involved in the festival," the chief said.

"Every person except the chief of police and the mayor."

"But, Dad, we just don't want to—"

"No, buts!" my father, the mayor said, cutting me off.

"And don't even think of saying anything either," the chief, Keegan's dad said, shooting him a serious look.

"We both feel that it's important for the two of you to learn about responsibility," my father said.

"Isn't trying to *make* us responsible sort of like *volunteering* us?" I asked.

"He's right," Keegan agreed. "And, even if he wasn't, how is dressing up in the Stewie the Tomato mascot suit going to make us more responsible?"

"Nobody said anything about dressing up as mascots," the chief said. "We want you to be doing something more visible."

"Like what?" Keegan asked.

"What do *you* want to do?" the chief asked.

"Well...the beauty pageant wouldn't be the worst place in the world to—"

"No beauty pageant," I said, cutting him off.

"I wasn't serious about you competing in the beauty pageant," Keegan said.

"I just thought we could do something else," I said.

Actually I hadn't, but Keegan's ex-girlfriend, Kelsey, was entered in the pageant. Putting him anywhere near her right now would be a big mistake.

"So, what did you have in mind?" my father asked.

Now I had to come up with something. I quickly tried to figure out which event or activity was the *least* lame. It was almost a tie for last place. Then I remembered something even better—one of the regular events had been canceled this year. Perfect, volunteer for something that isn't happening.

"Um...I don't know...maybe something to do with the tomato toss."

That was an event where people paid a quarter and were given a tomato to toss at a target.

"We weren't planning on running that event this year," my father said.

"No tomato toss!" Keegan exclaimed. "If

there isn't a tomato toss I'm not sure I even want to *go* to the festival. I think that we should boycott the whole thing as a form of protest against it not being run this—"

"The tomato toss is back in," the chief said.

"I agree," my father said. "But since we're putting it in just for you two that means you won't just be *working* that event, you'll be *organizing* it."

A combination of my terrible suggestion and Keegan's big mouth had made a bad situation worse. There had to be some way out of it.

"Well," I began, "if we run the event, then we should decide what to do with the money it makes."

"Alex, we can't just let you have the money," my father scoffed.

"Not keep it for us, but use it...use it to um...fix up the skate park."

I knew how much both of them hated skateboarding and the skate park.

"You already have two of those ramps and a bar thing," the chief said.

"It's called a rail, and we have two old, handmade, wooden ramps," Keegan explained. "Our skate park is a joke."

Of course, it was a joke because of the way our fathers felt about it.

"And you want to raise money to fix it up?" my father said.

"We do. Wouldn't that show responsibility?" I asked.

"It would, but it's a lot of work to run an event," he replied.

"We'd get some help," I said.

"Most people are already committed to something. Getting help won't come easy," my father warned.

"We can get our friends to help," I suggested. "Like we said, none of them are doing anything."

"And they would probably like to keep it that way," Keegan suggested.

"We could convince them," I said.

Keegan smiled. "We probably could. Especially if we could promise them new equipment."

"I'm not sure having your friends

involved would be helpful," my father said.

"How about David and Sam?" I suggested, pulling out my aces in the hole again.

"Well...the two of them would help make it work," he admitted. "They're very responsible young men. The two of you could learn from them."

What I knew we *could* learn was how to do wrong things and never get caught. They had an amazing ability to always come out looking innocent.

I stopped myself from smiling. I reached out my hand. "So, do we have a deal?"

He reached to shake, and I suddenly pulled mine away.

"But the deal is that *we* get to decide how we run it, who else we run it with, and there's no outside interference...from anybody, including the two of you," I said, pointing at our fathers.

"That would show responsibility," Keegan added.

My father looked like he was going to argue but he didn't. "Agreed."

We shook on it.

"All settled," the chief said.

"There, now that wasn't so hard, was it?" my father asked.

"Not that hard," I agreed.

"Oh, by the way, speaking of hard," the chief said. "Have you finished doing the jobs you were given?" he asked Keegan.

Keegan's dad was not just the chief of police. He was also a tomato grower, and Keegan often had work to do around the farm.

"Not everything, but it'll be done before you get home," Keegan said. "Alex even offered to help."

I tried to hide my look of surprise. Where was I when I agreed to that?

"That's nice of you," the chief said.

"It's the least I could do," I said. What I wanted to say was "What are you talking about, Keegan?" but I didn't.

Keegan just smiled—that same smirky, evil-genius smile of his that I knew so well.

chapter three

We left the office. We dropped our skateboards to the ground, pushed off and started gliding.

"Volunteering for something that was cancelled was a stroke of genius," Keegan said.

"Thank you."

"Shame it didn't work. Maybe it would have been smarter to just not say anything."

"Yeah, like you could do that," I said.

"But you know we weren't leaving that office without having to do something."

"Yeah, but something is a lot different than having to be responsible for running an entire event."

"It's not a big event. We just have to put up a few targets, get some tomatoes delivered and take the money. It's pretty simple."

"And boring."

"As opposed to dressing up in the mascot outfit or being part of the parade?" I questioned. "Or were you hoping to enter the Leamington Idol contest? I was really looking forward to hearing you sing."

"You won't catch me up on stage singing," Keegan said.

"That's good news for the dogs in town," I said.

The Leamington Idol contest was like a small town *American Idol* where people got up to sing in front of the whole town on the main stage. Some of the performers were actually pretty good.

Unfortunately *everybody* thought they

could sing. And when they got up on stage they often proved that theory wrong.

"What was wrong with my suggestion to help with the beauty pageant?" Keegan asked.

"Do you think that you and Kelsey in the same place is a good idea?"

"I'm positive it's a *great* idea."

"And I'm sure both she and her new boyfriend would disagree."

"I don't care what he thinks...actually I don't believe he *does* think. The guy is such a caveman. He operates on only basic instincts. Ug...Owen...need meat...Owen need fire...fire *magic*."

"You be sure to do that impersonation the next time you see Owen. He'll be really impressed."

"I would, but he wouldn't understand that I was insulting him. I just can't believe that she dumped me for a tuba player. Can you believe that, a *tuba* player!"

"First off, she didn't dump you. You told her that you wanted to see other people."

"Yeah, *I* wanted to see other people.

That didn't mean I wanted *her* to see other people."

"Okay, I'm not even going to go there. Second, you didn't even seem interested in her until she started to see somebody else."

"She's not just seeing somebody else, she's seeing a *tuba* player. The freak plays tuba in a marching band. Who in their right mind dates a tuba player?"

"Certainly a step down from you," I said, "but he does do a few other things too."

"There's only a few other things that stand in the way of me kicking the stuffing out of him!"

"And would those include the fact that he out-weighs you by sixty pounds, plays on the football team and is the state wrestling champion?"

"Those would be the things," Keegan admitted. "As well, I pride myself on being nonviolent."

"Especially when you're on the receiving end of the violence."

"Especially correct. You know he's all wrong for her. For one thing he's just *way* too old. Seniors shouldn't be allowed to date sophomores. He's almost three years older than her."

"If you mean three years, as in she's just about to turn sixteen and he's just about to turn eighteen, then you should check your math."

"Shows how little you know. He turns eighteen two weeks before she turns sixteen so that means for those two weeks he *will* be three years older than her."

"I stand corrected, although I'm a little stunned that you know his birthday. Were you planning to get him something?"

"Yeah, right. I just know his birthday. And it's not only that it's three years, it's a percentage thing. He's like...like...what percent older is he than Kelsey?"

"Twenty percent," I said.

"Are you sure it isn't more?"

"Are you questioning my math ability?" I asked.

He shook his head. "You are Mr. Math.

But really, there's got to be some law against it."

"You might want to check with your father on that one. He probably would have arrested him by now if that was a problem."

"I'll check with him. I know that in some states it must be illegal to date somebody who's twenty-percent younger than you."

"I doubt it."

"Then if it isn't illegal, it should at least be *immoral*...sort of like dating your cousin."

"In some states I think it's illegal *not* to date your cousin," I joked, "but I don't think this is one of those states. If it would make you feel any better we could paint his face on one of the targets and you could toss tomatoes at it."

"I'd rather toss tomatoes at him."

"Safer to toss at the targets," I said. "And just remember we'll be making some money to fix up the skate park."

"Do you really think we could raise enough money to buy anything worth having?" Keegan questioned.

"Any money is better than no money."

"I guess you have a point," he said. "It just seems like a lot of work."

"Speaking of work, everybody wants to volunteer me to do work today. What exactly did you volunteer me to do at your farm?" I asked.

"It's nothing," said Keegan.

"If it's nothing, you can do it by yourself. Tell me what it is."

"It'll take fifteen, twenty minutes at most. It's nothing."

"Tell me exactly what this nothing is or it'll take you exactly twice as long to do it by yourself."

"We just have to move some tomatoes," Keegan explained. "Some rotten tomatoes out of storage and into the compost, that's all."

"Sounds delightful."

"Not delightful, but we'll both get paid and that's not bad."

"Not bad," I agreed.

We came to a stop at the lights and jumped off our boards. My board skittered away to the side. For a second I thought I was going to trip before I regained my balance.

"Mind if I ask you a question?" Keegan asked.

"Could I stop you if I wanted?"

He shook his head. "Probably not. I was just wondering, why do you want to raise money to improve the skate park?"

"I just want to make it better."

"Yeah, that's great. It's just...you're not really a very good skateboarder."

"I'm not fantastic, but it's not like I'm the worst person in the world."

"Not the worst," he agreed. "But the person who's had the worst luck with injuries."

"I haven't been injured in weeks."

He pointed down at my left leg which was all ripped up on the outside of the calf.

"Okay, I haven't been injured badly in *almost* a week. So, what's your point?"

"It is just that people usually only like what they are good at, but you love skateboarding."

"And because I'm not that good you don't think I should like it so much?"

He shrugged. "I guess. I gotta give you credit though. Nobody, and I mean nobody, can take the pain and abuse you suffer and keep coming back for more."

"I guess that's a compliment."

"It is, man, believe me," said Keegan. "You're like a superhero with absolutely *no* powers. Forget Superman or Spiderman or Batman. They have special powers or abilities or at least really, really cool utility belts. But *you*—you know you can't fly but you keep jumping off those buildings. Now that takes guts."

"Guts or stupidity."

"Wasn't going to mention that, but maybe both. You're like my personal superhero... Splatman!"

"You make it sound like I never land a trick," I said.

"You land some, but *not* landing them doesn't seem to stop you. Me, if I missed a trick six or seven dozen times I might just stop. But you, you just keep coming."

"Again, I'll take that as a compliment."

"It *is*, believe me."

"And I guess we're very similar that way," I said.

"We are?" Keegan asked, looking confused. He was a great boarder and hardly ever missed a trick.

"Yeah. How many times in the last month has Kelsey said no to getting back together with you?"

"More than I can count."

"But you still keep picking yourself off the ground, wiping away the humiliation and coming back for more, knowing that she wants you to die," I said.

"It isn't that bad."

"Oh, it is," I said. "Believe me, it is. But still, you haven't given up."

"Not yet. I remain hopeful."

"Hard to see how. It isn't like she's given you even a word of encouragement."

"But there is encouragement. It's like I said...she's dating a *tuba* player. Sooner or later she'll have to come to her senses."

chapter four

I dug the shovel into the pile of rotting tomatoes, and they dripped and dropped into the wheelbarrow. The tomatoes looked disgusting and smelled worse. They were all rotting and running and looked more like blood and gore than produce. It all reminded me of an episode of *CSI* or the *Texas Chainsaw Massacre*.

I dropped the shovel and picked up the now-full wheelbarrow. Carefully I pushed it out of the barn. This was my sixth load and I was really working up a sweat...which reminded me...where exactly was Keegan? He said he was just going to the bathroom and, unless he was actually having a bath, he should have been back by now.

Then I saw him. He was sitting on a stump in the shade, talking on the phone. His wheelbarrow was still filled with tomatoes. In the time I'd dumped the last two loads he still hadn't emptied one.

"Keegan!" I called out.

He turned around, scowled and gestured for me to leave him alone. Then he turned his back to me and kept talking on the phone.

I felt my temper starting to rise. This wasn't even my job to begin with and now I was the only one working. I was getting so mad that I could just...I looked down at the tomatoes in my wheelbarrow.

I reached down and picked up one of the tomatoes. It was so overripe it was squishy and soft to the touch. My fingers sunk in, almost breaking the skin. I tossed it a few inches up into the air and caught it again. Nice weight. Nice.

Keegan still had his back to me. There was a slight wind—left to right—so I'd have to take that into account. I drew my arm back and threw the tomato. It flew through the air, slightly spiraling, toward him and— Splat! It smashed right into the back of his head and exploded into a thousand pieces of pulp!

Keegan shrieked and jumped into the air, spinning around in mid-flight. His expression was shock, fear and confusion, all rolled into one. He didn't know what had happened.

He reached up to the back of his head. When his hand came back covered with tomato he quickly put the pieces together in his head. There was only me here, standing in front of a wheelbarrow full of rotten tomatoes.

I started to laugh so hard that I almost fell over. Keegan's expression wasn't so joyful. He hung up the phone and slipped it into his pocket.

Suddenly he broke into a smile. That wasn't the reaction I expected.

"Lucky shot," Keegan said.

"Lucky for me."

"*Completely* lucky. You don't throw much better than you board. One-in-a-million shot. I could stand here all day, and you wouldn't be able to do that a second time."

I picked up a second tomato. "Wanna find out?"

"Go ahead."

"Turn around again. I don't want you to move if it's coming for you."

He started to turn around and then stopped and spun back around to face me. "But, first I should get a shot at you. That would be fair...right?"

I shrugged. I had to admit that it did seem fair. "Go for it."

"You turn around."

Reluctantly I turned. It was better to get it in the back of the head instead of in the face—not that he was going to hit me. It *was* a pretty lucky shot that I got him to begin with. I doubted he could hit me.

"Go ahead and throw the—"

A tomato flew by my head, missing by at least two feet. I knew he couldn't hit me. A second tomato crashed into the back of my head and I screamed in shock and pain. It really hurt! As I turned around, a third tomato whizzed by my face, just barely missing my nose.

"Hey, you were only supposed to—" Another tomato was midair, and I ducked behind my wheelbarrow as it flew past.

I grabbed a tomato and flung it wildly at him, missing by a mile. I grabbed another and took aim, and it smashed into the side of his wheelbarrow.

Keegan grabbed an armful of rotten tomatoes and started running directly at me. I pitched one high and wide and then a second that was a direct hit, square in the middle of his chest!

He staggered slightly, slowed down and then dodged to the side. I hurled another tomato, but it missed—he was practically on top of me. I reached down and grabbed two handfuls of rotten tomato pieces and flung them in his face at the same instant he threw his armful of tomatoes at me. I had just enough time to close my eyes as they exploded into my face, temporarily blinding me.

I reached over, grabbed Keegan by the shirt and tried to pull him forward and into the wheelbarrow. He fought back, and he was bigger than me. He reached down and scooped out more tomatoes, throwing them up into my face. This wasn't working at all.

Still holding his shirt tightly in my hands I threw myself backward. My weight pulled him forward, depositing him in the wheelbarrow. The tomatoes squashed under him and overflowed over the sides of the wheelbarrow and onto me!

I tried to roll out of the way but before I could get away the wheelbarrow tipped over and I was covered by tomatoes and Keegan.

"Truce, truce!" Keegan screamed as he rolled off me.

"Truce," I agreed.

Keegan's hair and face, pants and shirt were red and pulpy. He looked like he'd been shot in a dozen places, bloody and gory.

"You know who you look like?" Keegan asked.

"You?"

"With your hair color and freckles, plus all the tomato pieces and your shirt stained red you look like Stewie the Tomato," he said.

"Then that makes two of us," I said. "You should look at yourself!"

He held up a red hand and then looked down at himself.

"Okay, me too. But you gotta admit that *was* fun."

"I liked it. Especially the first shot. It was pretty cool to aim at a real live target."

"It was," he agreed. "I'd pay money to do that."

"So would I."

"In that case, maybe instead of getting paid to help, you should pay me for the privilege of tossing tomatoes," Keegan suggested.

"Yeah, this was a lot more fun than tossing

them at some stupid target—" Suddenly an idea came to me.

"It's not just you or me who would pay money for this. I bet a whole lot of people would pay a lot of money to throw a tomato at a real live person."

Keegan smiled. "Are you saying what I think you're saying?"

I nodded. "Forget targets. Let's charge people to throw tomatoes at other people."

"Come on," Keegan said. "You can't believe that they'd let us do that."

"What's the difference between throwing tomatoes at a target and throwing them at people?" I asked.

"Well, one is definitely more fun. But I'm willing to bet that our fathers won't see it that way."

"I don't see how they *can* object," I said. "Didn't they say we're in charge? That we get to make the decisions? That we're responsible?"

"I heard all of those things," he agreed. "But that doesn't mean they won't stop us."

"I know one way to *guarantee* that they won't say no."

"You do?"

"Yeah. We don't ask. We just do."

"I like the way you think," Keegan said.

"You mean you like the way I scheme."

"That's what I meant."

"We have two weeks before the festival, two weeks to put everything together," I said.

"And two weeks for the secret to get out."

"Only way to keep it secret is to keep it between us. We can't even tell David or Sam."

"They keep their mouths shut."

"We'll tell them the day of the festival. The less people who know, the better. We tell nobody...not even old girlfriends."

"Come on, give me some credit. I'm not completely stupid...not completely."

"When you're around her, I'm not so sure. Nobody. Agreed?"

"Agreed." He gave me his famous smile. "This is going to be so cool."

chapter five

When the singer hit the last note of her song her voice broke. Across town dogs were hiding under beds, paws pressed to ears. The audience clapped and cheered as the music ended. I didn't think they were impressed with her voice, just glad it was over. She bowed and waved as she bounced off the stage.

"Let's give it up for little Melissa Ellis!" the announcer yelled into the microphone, and people cheered some more.

I clapped as well—it would have been mean not to cheer for a six-year-old brave enough to get up on a stage and sing in front of hundreds of people. Of course it would have been better if she was the only six-year-old who was trying. It was like they'd cleared out a whole elementary school and brought them all here to perform.

"Is this getting worse every year or is it just me?" Keegan asked.

"Some of the singers are still really good, it's just that it seems like there's more that are worse."

"Don't they hold auditions, or do they just let anybody in?"

"Pretty well anybody," I said.

"Next up," the announcer said, "is a regular here at the Leamington Idol contest, Bert Conroy and his accordion!"

"I'm outta here," Keegan said as he got to his feet.

I followed as the audience cheered and Bert started playing. Bert was a teacher at our school and, thank goodness, he was a better teacher than accordion player.

We shuffled through the crowd, out of the tent and into the display area. There was booth after booth selling crafts. Just how many dream catchers, necklaces and black velvet pictures of Elvis did anybody want or need?

"I can't believe how crowded this place is," Keegan said.

"Pretty sad. Not much here that I want."

"Well, I can see one thing I definitely want."

"Are you thinking about the ribs?" I asked, pointing to where they were holding a rib-off contest. "Actually, her ribs aren't even close to her best feature."

Up ahead I saw Kelsey walking along eating an ice cream. What I didn't see was her boyfriend, Owen, but I knew he wouldn't be far away.

"I'm going to talk to her," Keegan said.

I grabbed him by the arm. "How about if we just go for ribs instead? My treat."

"Talk first. Eat later."

I let go of his arm. There was no point

in fighting this unless I was going to drag him away.

"Come on, Keegan, what's the point? She doesn't want to talk to you."

"I'll talk. She can listen."

"Owen isn't going to like you doing this."

"I don't care what he likes."

The smart thing would be to walk in the other direction. I wasn't that smart.

She moved toward us along the path. As she walked she talked to different people—like everybody else, she knew more than half the people in the park. I watched as she walked, laughing, smiling—Kelsey did have an incredible smile. Of course that smile would shut down pretty quick once she saw Keegan on the path and—she saw him, saw us. For a split second she hesitated and then kept moving.

"Hello, Alex," she said as she came close.

"Hey, Kelsey."

"No hello for me?" Keegan asked.

"I have no nothing for you," she said coldly as she walked past.

Keegan nudged me in the side. "Say something," he hissed.

"Where are you going?" I asked.

She turned around. "Leamington Idol."

"We were just heading that way," I said. "Mind if we join you?"

"I don't mind if *you* join me," she said and kept walking.

"Come on," Keegan said to me. "That was sort of an invitation."

We trotted down the path and caught up to her.

"Where's the boyfriend?" Keegan asked.

She ignored him.

"Where is Owen today?" I asked.

"He's meeting me at the talent tent later on."

"Great, so we have a little time to talk before he comes," Keegan said.

"I have no time for you."

"You can't stay mad at me forever," Keegan said.

"Forever is a long time. I was thinking no more than fifty years." She started walking away again.

"That's encouraging," Keegan whispered to me.

"How is that encouraging?"

"Last week she told me it would a hundred years before she'd talk to be again. At this rate she'll be talking to me in no time!" Keegan said. "Come on!"

He went after her, and I hurried to catch up to him.

"Say something else to her," Keegan hissed.

Something else...what did he want me to say?

"Kelsey!" I called out, and she turned around yet again.

"Are you coming to the tomato toss tomorrow?" I asked.

"I'm not sure. Depends how things go in the Miss Tomato Festival."

"Yeah, good luck with that."

"She won't need luck to win," Keegan said.

Her face softened. She looked like she

was almost going to smile, but she stopped herself.

"We're running the tomato toss this year," I said.

"You are?" She sounded genuinely surprised—not that I blamed her.

"Yeah, we wanted to be more responsible," I said.

"I can see you doing that," she said. "But other people feel that they're not responsible for anything they do," she said, shooting darts at Keegan with her eyes.

"People change," Keegan said.

"People, yes. You, no."

Kelsey walked into the tent. Owen stood up and waved, and she went over to his table. She greeted him with a kiss, and I could almost feel Keegan shudder.

"I just can't believe she's with him," he said. "Beauty and the tuba player."

"And there's nothing you can do about it."

"I should just walk over there and pop him one in the face!" Keegan said.

"You can't just walk up to somebody in

the middle of the Leamington Idol contest and hit him. Do you know how much trouble you'd be in?"

"Okay, you're probably right. Taking a shot at him there would be stupid."

"Taking a shot at him anywhere would be stupid, but right there, right now, would be *incredibly* stupid, even by your standards."

For a split second he looked like he was going to argue, but he didn't.

"Okay, that would be stupid, but I'd love to have a chance to take him on, one-on-one, away from the crowd and witnesses."

Then, just like he was listening to what had just been said, Owen stood up and walked out of the tent.

"I wonder where he's going?" I asked.

"Only one way to find out."

Keegan started off at a trot, and I ran to catch up.

"What are you doing? You can't really be thinking about fighting him, can you?"

"Just come on."

Again I followed. We circled the big tent and started down the path. It was darker away from the lights and, except for a man walking along the path toward the tent, completely deserted.

"Why would he be going down here?" I asked.

"Look, port-a-potties," Keegan said.

There were five blue port-a-potties peeking through the trees.

"That explains why he's down here."

"This has potential," Keegan said.

"Him going to the washroom has potential?"

"Maybe. Do you have a pen?"

I did have a pen. I'd been using it to make last-minute notes about the tomato toss. I pulled it out of my pocket and handed it to him.

"What are you going to do, write him a nasty note?" I asked.

"Haven't you heard that the pen is mightier than the sword?"

"I'd feel better if you had a sword."

"Come on."

Keegan ran along the path, and I trailed after him. I couldn't see how this could end well, but I was way too curious to be reasonable. What was he up to?

Keegan stopped at the first port-a-potty and pulled open the door. It was empty. He did the same with the second—also empty.

He grabbed the third door.

"It's occupied!" called out a voice—Owen's booming voice!

Keegan looked at me and smiled. He then took the pen and slipped it into the little bracket on the door—he was using the pen to lock Owen inside the toilet! Owen was going to be stuck in a toilet...at least until he pressed hard enough to break the pen.

"Come on," I whispered. "We have to leave."

"We have one more thing to do first," Keegan whispered back.

He put his hands against the front of the port-a-potty. What was he going to? Then it came to me.

The five toilets were perched at the top of a little hill leading down to the beach. He was trying to push it over and down

the hill! Unbelievable, crazy, dangerous...
brilliant!

I put my hands against it as well.

"Let's do it," Keegan mouthed.

Together we pushed, and the toilet lifted
slightly off the ground.

"Hey!" Owen yelled from inside.

I jumped away in shock, and the whole
thing thumped back onto the ground. We
had to get out of here before he broke the
pen and found out it was us! I started to
run, and Keegan grabbed my arm and shook
his head violently. He wasn't going to leave.
This was going to end up in a fight!

He pushed against the port-a-potty
throwing his whole body against it. It
started to rise off the ground again, and
Owen started screaming. It was balanced
on edge. I could see the strain in Keegan's
face. He was pushing for all he was worth,
but he couldn't quite make it tip, and he
couldn't hold it for much longer. There was
only one thing to do.

I threw my body against it as well, and
it kept rising and rising! I could hear the

sewage sloshing around inside. The stinking smell rose up, and Owen screamed louder and louder. And the toilet toppled over backwards!

It fell with a thud and started to slide down the hill, gaining speed, sewage surging out, until it shuddered to a stop at the bottom!

"Now we run!" Keegan said.

chapter six

"Stop running!" I said to Keegan as I grabbed his arm to slow him down.

"He'll kill us if he catches us."

"That's why we have to slow down. We don't want to run into the tent looking guilty. We have to look casual."

"Good point," he said.

We walked—quickly—and the tent came into view. We'd been able to hear the singer all the way down at the port-a-potties. She was pretty good, which was lucky for us, because people were watching her. Nobody saw us enter the tent. We eased into the back of the crowd just as her song ended and we joined the crowd in cheering.

"Way to go!" I screamed. "Wasn't she something!" I said to the two women standing beside us. "She was the best!"

"That's our niece," one of the women said proudly.

"You tell her that I think she should win the contest. She is amazing, like her next step should be *American Idol*!"

Both women flashed big smiles. "Thank you so much, that's so kind of you," the other woman said.

Keegan turned so he faced away from them and gave me a "what are you doing?" look.

"Alibi," I mouthed.

He nodded, and I could see the flash of understanding cross his face. He turned back to the women.

"I'm Keegan and this is Alex. You be sure to tell your niece that we enjoyed every single note. When she started so strong I thought there was no way she could top that. But she just got better and better. What a performance!"

"Well, Keegan and Alex, I'll be sure to pass your compliments on to Mandy and—" She stopped mid-sentence, and her eyes got big. "Oh my goodness."

I turned around. I saw Owen charging toward the tent. He was covered, head to toe, with sewage—his clothes, his hair, his face, everything. But through it all I could see the anger on his face. He looked like a big, stinking bull!

Part of me wanted to laugh, but the other part wanted to run away. He looked so incredibly angry and he had to know it was us.

He locked his eyes on us and stomped forward, the look of anger giving way to complete rage.

"Whoa, what happened to you?" Keegan asked him.

"You know what happened!" he screamed. Dozens of people all around turned to face him and us.

"All I know is you have to work on your toileting habits," Keegan said. "I thought by your senior year you'd be potty trained."

He skidded to a stop just a few feet away. The smell was overwhelming!

"You're going to pay for this!" he bellowed. "Let's go, right now! Let's go!"

"I'm not going anywhere with you," Keegan said. "At least until you clean up a little. You might want to start by removing the toilet paper from your head."

There was a strip of used toilet paper fluttering down one side of his head. My stomach did a flip as he pulled it off and it stuck to his hand. He shook it back and forth before it fell to the ground.

"What exactly is happening here?"

I turned around. It was Clyde and Bonnie. The crowd, which had gathered around us, separated to let them through. I don't think I'd ever been so glad to see them in my entire life.

"I'll tell you what happened!" Owen screamed. "Somebody pushed a port-a-potty down a hill when I was inside!"

The whole crowd broke into laughter, and Owen looked even angrier. I started to laugh as well—I didn't want to, but I just couldn't stop myself.

"He's crazy," Keegan said. "I didn't do anything."

"I know you did it!" he bellowed.

"Keep your voice down," Clyde said. "Try to stay calm."

"Yeah, stay calm. We wouldn't want you to get so excited that you wet yourself or...I guess it's too late for that."

"You're dead, you stupid little—"

"Nobody is going to threaten anybody around here," Clyde said, cutting him off.

"Then I want him arrested. You can't just go around doing this to people, can you?" Owen demanded.

"No, sir. That would be public mischief and possibly even common assault," Bonnie said. "Did you see him push the toilet over?"

"Of course not. It's not like they have windows, you know!"

"No need to be sarcastic with me, son. Did anybody see him do it?"

"It's not like I talked to anybody. I just crawled out of the toilet."

"So it just happened," Clyde said.

"Just now. Just this minute."

"And I was right here for the last five minutes," Keegan said.

"Do you have anybody who can vouch for your whereabouts?" Clyde asked.

"He was with me the whole time," I said— and that wasn't even a lie.

"He's just lying for his friend!" Owen bellowed.

"I have friends who *would* lie for me," Keegan said. Then he realized what he had just said. "Not that he *is* lying or anything."

"Is there anybody else who can tell us that you were here the whole time?" Clyde asked. "Somebody a little more impartial."

"We can," one of the women said, stepping forward. "These two very kind boys were right here beside us, listening to my niece sing."

"Sing like an angel," I added. "Mandy was the highlight of the entire evening."

"And they were here?" Clyde asked. "You'd testify to that?"

"Are you questioning my word?" the woman asked, sounding offended.

"Of course not, Ma'am!" Clyde said. "I just need to make sure that you definitely saw them."

"I most certainly did."

"As did I," the second woman added.

"Thank you...both of you," Clyde said. "Let me just take down your information in case we need to investigate further."

Owen shot Keegan a look of complete and utter hatred.

"You really do stink," Keegan said. "You might want to think about changing deodorants."

"You think this is over?" Owen asked Keegan. "You can be as brave as you want now. Tomorrow is another day."

Suddenly Kelsey pushed through the crowd. When she saw Owen covered with sewage, she gasped and then gagged. Owen saw her and then turned and quickly ran away without saying a word.

Keegan walked over to her. "At least with me the crap is only on the inside."

chapter seven

I dropped the basket on the ground, and one of the tomatoes fell off the top and rolled away across the pavement.

"Be careful with the merchandise," Keegan said as he bent down and picked it up.

"These are really nice tomatoes."

"They're too rotten to eat, even too rotten to make ketchup out of, but just about perfect for tossing."

Keegan turned and threw the tomato

against the wall of the school. It splattered into a thousand little pieces and left a red stain on the wall.

"This is so cool. Where else can we throw a rotten tomato at somebody?"

I looked around. We'd transported the skateboard ramps from the park and had placed them at the far side of the school-yard. There were an even fifty bushels of tomatoes. A lot more than anybody had ever needed for the tomato toss, but nobody had ever done it this way before. The tomatoes were right beside the entrance. Everybody who paid would get ten tomatoes to throw.

This was the perfect place to run it. It was on the main street, but the yard was completely fenced in. The only way in was through the one gate, so we could control admission. David and Sam were sitting at the table by the gate.

We decided that we'd let in ten people at a time, and each person would have five minutes to fire.

"I believe we're ready."

"Shall we let the first group in?"

There was already a crowd waiting.

I looked at my watch. It was still a few minutes before nine, and technically, we weren't supposed to start things up until nine and..."Let's just do it."

We'd let word get out last night at the festival tent that we were going to be doing the tomato toss in a whole new way. We didn't say exactly how but promised it would be pretty exciting.

"Just how much money do you think we're going to make?" Keegan asked.

"No way of telling exactly."

"Then give me an inexact number."

I looked at the bushels of tomatoes.

"Well, there are fifty bushels and if each bushel holds approximately two hundred and fifty tomatoes, then we have twelve thousand, five hundred tomatoes. At two dollars for ten tomatoes, if we use up all the tomatoes we stand to make five thousand dollars."

"Come on, really?"

"Why do you ever doubt my excellent math skills?"

"I don't," he said, holding his hands up. "It's just that that's a whole lot of money."

"It is, but if we end up with nothing but empty bushels that's what we'll make."

"Then let's start making money."

Keegan went over and helped David and Sam collect money and escort the first group in. Kids pushed and shoved and laughed as they came in.

"So, you ready?" Keegan asked.

"As ready as I'm going to be."

We'd drawn numbers and I'd lost. I was the first human target. I grabbed my board and walked over to the space between the two ramps.

"Okay?" Keegan yelled out.

I pulled on my helmet and nodded. I ran and jumped on my board, shooting across the open space between the two ramps, directly in front of the people with the tomatoes.

Almost instantly they started throwing tomatoes at me. There was a rush of red as tomatoes flew through the air and by my head, hit the ramps and the ground, sailed high and wide and hit the side of the school. But not one hit me as I rolled behind the second ramp, safe and sheltered! Every single tomato had missed! I started to laugh.

"Can't any of you throw at all?" Keegan yelled. "Get ready, he's coming back for another pass!"

As I stood up, getting ready to make a run, a tomato hit the side of my helmet, little bits splattering into my face.

A roar went up from the crowd and the kids in the throw zone.

I ducked down again, safe for a few seconds. I wiped the tomato off my face.

"Come on!" Keegan yelled.

I stayed low, took a run and jumped on the board, pushing off hard to gain as much speed as possible. The tomatoes came flying, landing all around. Then I was hit on the side, and another tomato smashed against my leg. A third hit me on the foot. I sailed across the opening and then almost fell off the board as I reached the safety of the ramp. The last few tomatoes splattered against it.

I peeked around the ramp. Some of the kids had started walking toward the gate. They were empty-handed, out of ammunition. The rest were just standing there, hands at their sides. They had all run out of tomatoes. That wasn't so bad, I thought. I had a couple of stains on my clothes, but no serious damage.

I grabbed the board and started to walk away when I was hit squarely in the shoulder by a tomato. I looked over at the kids. One of them bowed gracefully from the waist. Apparently there had been *one* more tomato.

"That was pretty cool," Keegan said.

"It'll be even cooler when it's your turn."

"But not as much fun for the people tossing the tomatoes."

"How do you figure that?"

"With the speed I move, they won't be able to hit me."

"I guess we'll find out. Are you next?"

"No, first Dave, then Sam, then me."

"I can hardly wait. I might buy some tomatoes myself for that."

"Anything that raises more cash. Let's let in the next group."

I walked over to the fence and looked up and down the street.

"What are you looking for?" Keegan asked.

"Your father, my father, Owen. People who might cause trouble."

"You don't have to worry about any of them."

"I don't?" I asked.

"At least not until the parade is over. Both our fathers are busy getting everything organized, and Owen is part of the parade."

"That's right, he's in the marching band."

"He's the *tuba* player in the marching band," Keegan said. "If being in a marching band isn't lame enough, imagine being the tuba player in a marching band."

"Could be worse. Do they have accordion players?"

"That would be even cooler. We don't have to worry about anything until after the parade."

I looked at my watch. It was just after nine. The parade was scheduled to start at ten and would be over before eleven. We had two hours of peace. There was a loud whoop as another firefight of tomatoes began—at least relative peace.

"I'm not worried about our fathers," Keegan said. "By the time they even notice what we're doing they'll see we've made a wad of money."

"And Owen?"

"What's he going to do, fight me here in front of everybody?"

"He could."

"Let him show up. I'm armed and dangerous," Keegan said as he held up a tomato.

I was pretty sure that Keegan was just joking around...pretty sure.

chapter eight

I sat on my skateboard. My clothes, board and body were completely covered with tomato stains. Dave and Sam weren't much better. Keegan had been hit as well, but he wasn't nearly as coated.

The initial rush of customers had ended and there were only a few people waiting in line. I thought it was going to be just kids, but lots of adults had come to toss tomatoes as well. Right now the people waiting in line were all adults—well they were like twenty or so.

We were taking a short break. We needed a break—it hurt when a tomato caught you in the face, no matter how squishy it was. And twice I was knocked clear off my board and skidded into the pavement. A helmet and knee pads provided only so much protection.

"Parade is getting ready to start," I said.

"Always a highlight for me," Keegan replied.

"Really?"

"Yeah, right," he said.

I walked over to the fence and rested my arms on the top of it. The street was now blocked off, and there was no traffic. Along the sidewalk, on both sides, people were lining the route. There were whole families sitting together on the curb, older people with lawn chairs and coolers. There were clusters of older kids all standing around, trying to look like they weren't too interested—but they were here.

People were licking ice cream cones or eating hot dogs or drinking pop. A lot of people also had cameras and video recorders. That was stranger than just watching the parade—thinking that it was going to be so memorable that you'd want to capture it for later viewing. Unless those people had really low expectations, they were going to be deeply disappointed.

The local cable company was taping the whole thing as well. There were camera people situated along the parade route. That didn't say as much about the parade as about the fact that there was nothing else happening in town.

"I just can't believe that this parade draws such a big crowd," Keegan said.

"Year after year after year," I said.

"Pretty well everybody in town is here."

"Not just our town. My father told me that people come here just for the festival, book a hotel and stay for the weekend."

"Some people need to get a life," Keegan said. "Do you know what would really get an audience?"

I was almost afraid to ask.

"A contest where you push over port-a-potties," Keegan said.

"I'd pay to see that," David said with a laugh as he and Sam joined us at the fence.

"I guess the secret is convincing Owen to ever go inside one again," I added.

"No, that would be easy," David said. "Just have Keegan go inside, and Owen would follow. I get the feeling he's going to follow you everywhere until he finally catches you."

"Why does everybody think it was me?" Keegan asked.

Both David and Sam burst into laughter. "Like who else would be that stupid?" David asked.

"I prefer the term brave."

"No, he's right, stupid pretty well sums it up," I agreed.

"Well if *I'm* stupid then *you* were just as stupid."

"You?" David asked, pointing at me. "You helped push it over?"

"We're not admitting to anything," Keegan said. "But, *if* I did do it, and I'm not saying that I did, you know I'd need some help. Do you know how heavy those port-a-potties are? How hard they are to tip over?"

"I don't know...but apparently you do," David said.

"I knew it would be a two-man operation," said Sam.

David pointed at Keegan and then me, first holding up one finger and then a second, counting to two.

So much for *not* admitting to anything. Now it wouldn't just be Keegan that Owen would be searching for.

"How about if we just watch the parade?" I suggested.

"Maybe we should let the people waiting in line toss their tomatoes first," David said. "It looks like they're getting a little impatient."

I looked over. There were six of them. I didn't know any of them, and they looked a little rough around the edges—the sort of people I'd normally cross the street to avoid. They were also older—like in their early twenties.

"We're not supposed to run the event during the parade," I said.

"You go and tell them that," Keegan suggested.

"Sure." I walked over. As I got close I could swear that I smelled alcohol.

"It's about time," one of them said.

"You're going to have to wait a little bit longer. We're not allowed to run our event because of the parade," I said, trying to sound official and polite.

"I don't see no parade," one of them said. He sounded like he'd been drinking. It was still before ten in the morning. Who had something to drink this early in the day?

"It's just about to start. Tell you what, you can watch it from here, you can even have our chairs. And once it's over you can have twice as many tomatoes and twice as long for the same amount of money."

"Now that sounds like a deal," the same guy said. The others nodded in agreement.

Three of them took the chairs and the other three slumped down on the steps leading up to the schoolyard as I went back to join my friends.

"So, that was okay with them?" Keegan asked.

"Sure, no problem. Let's just watch the parade," I suggested.

"Sounds like you really want to see it," Keegan said.

"I've seen it fifteen times before and I'm sure there isn't going to be much different this time," I said.

"Can't imagine there will be *anything* different. At least business should pick up when the parade is over," Keegan said.

"Probably."

I heard the sound of bagpipes and looked up the street. There in the distance, way up the street, I could see the pipers. They always led the parade. Behind them I could make out the first cars—convertibles. My father, as mayor—would be in the lead car. That was tradition. The mayor always followed the pipers. Then the Miss

Tomato Festival contestants and then, in no particular order, a few tractors, some floats, guys on minibikes, some clowns, more floats, the high school marching band, some fancy cars and then, bringing up the rear, the fire trucks with their sirens blaring and bells ringing.

As they got closer the shrill sound of the pipers got louder and louder.

"You know," Keegan said. "There's only one thing worse than bagpipe music."

"Tuba music," I said.

"Yeah, exactly! That's the only thing that's worse."

"How much do you think somebody would pay to throw a tomato at one of the pipers?" I asked.

"Man, I know I'd pay a lot," David said.

Both Sam and Keegan agreed.

The pipers passed by and next in line—as always—was my father. He sat on the back of a convertible, waving and smiling at the crowd, the perfect politician.

Just then he looked over and saw the four of us covered in tomato stains. He froze, his hand above his head stuck in mid-wave, the smile replaced by a look of complete disbelief.

I didn't know whether I should be afraid or amused. I went with amused and waved back as his car rolled by. He cast one more glance over his shoulder, shook his head forlornly and then turned back to the crowd and started to wave. I couldn't see his face, but I knew he'd be smiling again.

I just wondered what was going on in his head. I guess I wouldn't have to wait long to find out. I was pretty sure he'd be back here as soon as the parade ended to tell me exactly what he thought. Maybe he wouldn't be pleased, but what could he really say? We were running the event and even making some money.

"There's my man!" Keegan yelled.

Next in line in the parade was Stewie The Tomato, the official mascot of the Tomato Festival. With him were his entire family—four other people dressed in tomato costumes to look like Mr. and Mrs.

Tomato and their three tomato children. They were riding atop a float that looked like a gigantic tomato basket.

"Hey, Stewie!" David yelled. "You rule, Stew!"

Stewie turned our way and waved. I noticed that the smile painted onto his costume looked very similar to the smile that my father was flashing. Maybe Stewie was thinking about running for mayor. He might have a shot.

"Anybody know who's inside the Stewie costume this year?" Keegan asked.

"No idea," I said. "I just know how hot he must be."

I'd been Stewie twice before and by the time they pulled the Stewie suit off me I was swimming in my own sweat. Not a pretty sight or smell—although compared to Owen last night I'd gotten off pretty easily.

Next in line came a float with an Elvis impersonator on the back. Music blared from the truck, and he sang along. When he wasn't being Elvis he ran the gas station.

He'd been a part of the parade for as long as I could remember.

He was dressed in a glitzy white jumpsuit covered in rhinestones and was wearing big, dark sunglasses and sideburns that were like pork chops.

Funny, he used to do a younger version of Elvis. Now he was imitating the middle-aged, big gut, eaten-too-many-donuts-and-deep-fried-chocolate-bars-and-cheesecake Elvis.

Right after Elvis came four white convertibles. Perched on the backseat of each were three of the contestants for the Miss Tomato Festival contest. All twelve contestants were dressed in identical long white dresses.

Kelsey sat in the second car, waving at people. If I had a vote she would have gotten it.

"She looks really good," I said without thinking.

"Sometimes you don't appreciate what you have until it's gone, huh, Keegan?" David asked. That was even worse than what I said.

"She's only gone for the moment. She'll come back to her senses."

"I don't know," David said. "I saw her and Owen together this morning down at the fairgrounds, and they were all kissy face and holding hands."

I cringed. This wasn't good—but maybe he needed to hear the truth.

"Hey, Kelsey!" Keegan yelled.

The three girls in her car looked over and all got that same stunned look that my father had when he saw us covered in tomato stains. Then they broke into big smiles and started laughing and pointing at us.

"I guess that's something," Keegan said. "I knew she couldn't stay mad at me forever."

"Just because she's laughing at you—laughing at all of us—doesn't mean she's going to forgive you," I said.

"Step by step, I'm moving in the right direction."

"Just don't forget that large roadblock and his tuba standing between you and her," I warned.

"I haven't forgotten. If it wasn't for that big goof everything would be fine by now."

"You can't blame him for everything."

"Of course I can. If I didn't, then I'd have to blame some of it on *me* and I'm not about to start doing that."

There was no point in saying anything more—reason hardly ever worked with Keegan.

"It's too bad we can't go to the beauty contest today," I said.

It was slated for the middle of the afternoon. We had to stay and run our event. Probably for the best because it would keep Keegan away from Kelsey and Owen.

The last of the convertibles passed by, and Kelsey continued along the parade route and away from us.

Next in line came the reason for the parade—actually the reason for the whole town being here. Two tractors slowly moved down the street. Each was pulling a gigantic trailer filled, almost overflowing, with field-ripe tomatoes. Kids dressed in red, ran beside the tractors and gave out candies to the kids sitting on the curb.

"And here comes your buddy," David said.

Right behind the tractor two girls held a large banner—*Leamington Heights Marching Band*, it proudly read.

Immediately behind the banner were the first members of the band—the majorettes. They were dressed, like everybody else in the band, in white and blue uniforms topped by blue cowboy hats trimmed with feathers. They all looked pretty ridiculous. The majorettes twirled and tossed their batons high into the air.

Next came the drummers—there were twenty of them at least—banging away, keeping a beat while the rest of the band followed, holding their instruments but not playing. Row after row, they marched forward. Clarinet players followed by the trumpets and trombones and then the two tuba players, Owen and some other poor sap, came next.

Suddenly the conductor yelled out a command, and all the instruments came to life in a rousing blaring version of a Beatles song. John, Paul, George and Ringo never would have written "Hey Jude" if they thought it was going to be played by a marching band.

As they closed in, the song got louder and louder. Once the row of trumpets had passed, the tuba players were so close that you could almost *feel* their playing and—a red blur flew across the street and slammed right into the big, upturned bell of Owen's tuba, disappearing inside!

Owen stumbled and stopped playing. He knew something had happened but he had no idea what it was.

I looked at Keegan. He was wide-eyed. He looked as shocked as Owen.

"I just...I just threw it...I wasn't thinking. I just—"

Then the six guys waiting in line started to toss tomatoes at the band too.

chapter nine

Tomatoes exploded against the members of the band! They startled and jumped, and a trumpet player dropped his trumpet. Some of them scrambled off to the side while others, not hit, not knowing what was going on, kept marching and playing. Owen stood there, stunned, holding his tuba. A tomato hit him squarely on his square head, and he stumbled backwards. Two more tomatoes hit him, and he ran away, using his tuba as a shield. Finally I'd found out what a tuba was good for.

Other tomatoes fell short of the band, hitting the people on the sidewalk. They screamed and scrambled out of the way.

A group of high school kids who had been watching, broke away and ran across the street, trying to get away from the fire—no, they ran up to the tomato trailer, grabbed tomatoes and returned fire!

The float following the band came into range. Suddenly the members of the local peewee baseball team were being fired on. They leaped off the float and ran for the tomato truck, grabbed tomatoes and started heaving them. In the confusion the baseball team didn't realize who was firing on them. They started to toss tomatoes at the teenagers who were doing battle with the six guys on the edge of the schoolyard. There was a gigantic food fight taking place right in front of us!

"We have to do something!" I screamed.

"You're right!" Keegan agreed.

He reached down and grabbed a tomato and tossed it at the six guys. David and Sam started to do the same thing. This wasn't what I had in mind. I grabbed the fence and leaped over it onto the sidewalk.

The whole street was going crazy. All up and down the parade route the madness was spreading.

The band had disintegrated. Its members had either run off or were holding their instruments in one hand and tossing tomatoes with the other. The baseball players were now showing why they were champions. They were working as a team, directing their fire at the original six shooters. Spectators had abandoned their seats, either running away or joining in the battle. There were lots of kids, but there were at least two senior citizens out there, their shirts stained with tomatoes, fighting back.

Another float cruised into the battle zone, and the choir from the local church came under fire. Tomatoes bounced off their white robes, and they screamed, stopped singing and abandoned the float.

Some of them ran toward another trailing tractor, towing another load of tomatoes. They started firing back, so much for turning the other cheek!

This was going from bad to worse. Where were the police, where was my father? He'd know what to do.

I started running up the street, but out in the open I was an instant target. I was pelted by tomatoes. They really stung as they hit. These weren't squishy rotten tomatoes but hard, good, eating tomatoes.

I dodged and wove, but I was hit by tomatoes on both sides. I wasn't getting away from them. The fight had already spread up the street, along the parade route.

Up ahead the four cars holding the Miss Tomato Festival contestants were under fire. Most of the girls ducked down in the convertibles, but the tomatoes kept coming, staining the white dresses with gigantic red welts.

Suddenly sirens started to blare. The street came alive with flashing lights and blaring horns. The police who had been blocking streets for the parade came running and driving onto the parade route.

A lot of people ran off, but unbelievably, others threw tomatoes at the police cruisers and the officers. They were in a firefight with cops. Were these people insane? They were using tomatoes against guys with guns and batons and pepper spray.

And that's when the fire department got involved. The big pumper truck roared up with water spewing out of its hoses. A thick stream of water shot out at a row of teenagers who hadn't given up the fight. It blew them backwards and onto their butts! They got up and ran off.

The firemen swung the hose around and aimed the jet of water at another stubborn pocket of people. They scattered and ran. The last few stragglers fled as the police spread out. It looked like it was finally over.

My father staggered up the street. His shirt was stained, tomato pieces dripped from his hair. He looked angrier than I'd ever seen him in my entire life.

Maybe this wasn't so much over as just beginning.

chapter ten

Once again we found ourselves sitting in my father's office. All around us were dozens of people, police and all of the members of the Tomato Festival committee. They were all yelling and screaming. It was almost as chaotic in here as it had been on the streets. The big difference was that nobody was throwing tomatoes, although there wasn't a single person in the room who didn't have at least one stain on their clothing.

Keegan and I were so covered that we

looked like we had one stain that covered our entire bodies. There was hardly any part of us that wasn't red and splattered. If the whole thing wasn't so serious it would have been funny.

Everybody was talking and yelling, but nobody seemed to be listening. I wanted to put my hands over my ears so I couldn't hear what they were talking about—who they were blaming—but I couldn't avoid hearing.

So far, thank goodness, nobody was pointing a finger directly at us, although there was a general sense that it had started somewhere near our event. It was also unsettling that we were the only kids in the room.

Keegan sat beside me, trying to look calm. It wasn't working. I knew him well enough to know that he was really, really worried. He was biting the inside of his lip, and his one foot was tapping like it had a life of its own.

He knew I wouldn't say a word, but I was sure that other people had seen him throw the first tomato. There were hundreds of people there when he started the riot.

Although, technically, Keegan hadn't really started it. He'd thrown that one tomato, but it hadn't hit anybody. It just disappeared into a tuba.

Everybody was so focused on the parade that maybe they hadn't noticed that first tomato—well, nobody but those guys waiting to toss tomatoes. They had seen him do it. I just hoped we'd seen the last of them.

Still, it was certain that lots of people saw where the first barrage came from—the tomato toss area. We were in charge, so that made us responsible. Denying would only work so far. It might be better to just admit that the whole thing was our fault. What was the worst they could do to us? No, I didn't want to think about that.

Thank goodness that at least it hadn't ruined the *whole* festival. Of course the parade had been stopped, and the beauty pageant was postponed until the contestants could change into something that didn't have tomato stains. I thought the stains would have made it a real Miss Tomato Festival contest in a bizarre way. But the rest of the events, all the booths and tents and the rides, were still going on as planned. Every event except the tomato toss. If that wasn't a statement of our guilt, I didn't know what was.

I could see out the window overlooking the main street. The fire department was out on the street right now. They'd finished hosing down the spectators and were now hosing down the street.

The police were there beside the firefighters, watching everybody and everything. It would be a certain arrest right now to even threaten to throw a tomato.

I'd overheard the chief tell my father that up to that point nobody had been arrested. I hoped we could keep it that way, although they really wouldn't arrest us for starting things...would they? I didn't want to put that to the test.

"Could I have everybody's attention, please!" my father said.

Either nobody heard him except me, or they were all too excited to listen.

"Everybody, shut up!" the chief yelled, and the room got silent. He turned to my father and motioned for him to speak.

"We need to stay focused," he said. "We still have a festival to run the rest of today and all of tomorrow. I need you all to go, get changed into different clothes if you have to and go down there and take charge of your events."

"You can't expect us to act like nothing happened," Mr. Miller, who ran the bank, said angrily. He had a large red stain on the back of his shirt. It looked like a bull's-eye.

"That's *exactly* what I want you to do. Go out and take care of things," my father said.

Mr. Miller had run against my father in the last election, and I knew the two men didn't like each other.

"We can't undo what's been done," my father said. "We can either sulk and complain or make it work. You do want to make it work, don't you?" he asked Mr. Miller.

"Of course I do. I just think that we have to get to the bottom of this."

"Believe me, I *am* going to get to the bottom of it," the chief said.

"Yes," my father agreed. "The chief and I will take personal responsibility to find out what happened, and more importantly, how to prevent it from happening again."

I was working hard at not making eye contact with anybody, but I thought some of the people in the room were looking at me and Keegan.

"But we need you all to go out there and make sure that everything else runs the way it's supposed to. Okay?"

There was a general nodding of heads and voicing of agreement.

"Thank you all," my father said. "Let's get going."

As people started out of the room Keegan and I got up as well, hoping to become lost in the crowd.

"Not you two," the chief said, and we both sat back down.

I had to fight the urge not to climb under the chair instead of sitting on it.

My father closed the door as the last person left. He took a chair, pulled it over until it was right in front of us.

"So, what happened?" he asked.

"It's really hard to say," I said.

"It just got so crazy so fast," Keegan agreed. "It was scary how quickly it spread."

"Yes it was. The big question isn't how fast it spread, but how it started in the first place. What sparked the fire?"

Keegan shrugged in response. I stayed quiet.

"Thank goodness nobody got hurt," my father said.

"There were a few bumps and bruises," the chief said.

"The big problem is that it's a major black eye for the festival and for the whole town," my father said.

"It's embarrassing," the chief agreed. "And you boys know nothing?"

I tried to look at him but found myself staring at my shoes.

"Maybe I should resign," the chief said.

"No way," Keegan said. "It wasn't your fault."

"My men couldn't get control at first," said the chief.

"But ultimately, it's my responsibility," my father said. "The buck stops at my desk. If anybody resigns it should be me. Somebody has to take responsibility for—"

"It's my fault," Keegan said, cutting him off.

My father and his father stared at him.

"It all happened because of me. I'm responsible."

"*We're* responsible," I added, before I could think to stop myself. "It all started with the tomato toss."

My father nodded. "We'd heard that it all started in the vicinity of your event."

"We closed it down because of the parade—the way we were supposed to—but there were these guys...we don't know who they are. They didn't want to wait and they started throwing tomatoes at the band."

"And then it just got crazy. We wanted to stop it but we couldn't," Keegan said. "But that isn't an excuse, it's my fault."

"*We're* responsible," I said.

Keegan stood up. "No, not *us*. It was me. *I* threw the first tomato."

Neither my father nor his father said a word. They looked shocked. I was shocked.

"It just happened. One second I'm holding a tomato and then the next I just threw it. I can't explain it," Keegan said.

"And that's where it's my responsibility," I said, jumping to my feet. "It was my idea to have the tomato toss with people as targets. If I hadn't done that, none of this would have happened. Not Keegan, not those guys, nothing. If you have to blame somebody, blame me."

"No, you can't blame Alex, he's just trying to defend me. It's my fault. Everything was under control until I threw the first tomato. It's all because of—"

"Both of you, stop!" my father ordered. "We need to discuss this. You two take a seat outside."

"Yes sir," I said dutifully. We shuffled to the reception area.

Mrs. Wallace was sitting at her desk watching TV—that was almost reassuring. She was the nerve center of the whole festival, and everybody phoned in to her to ask for information or updates about the events. Absently I started to watch TV—CNN *Headline News*. Maybe seeing a war somewhere else would make this seem less tragic.

"You didn't have to do that," Keegan said. "You didn't have to say it was your fault."

"Yes, I did. I'm as much to blame as you."

"Maybe more."

"What?" I exclaimed.

He smiled. "Just kidding. Thanks for sharing it."

"You know what they say, misery loves company. At least neither of us will be alone."

The door opened, and my father motioned

for us to come back in. We sat down again.

"We asked the two of you to get involved because we felt that you needed to be more responsible," the chief said.

"No argument from us about–"

"Close your mouth and quit interrupting!" the chief said, cutting Keegan off.

"Yes, sir."

"And we want to let you know that somehow, in some strange way, we're actually proud of you both," my father said.

"What?" I exclaimed.

"Despite knowing just how serious this is, you have accepted blame," my father said.

"You have claimed *responsibility* for your actions," the chief added. "You both really stepped up to the plate on this one."

I looked over at Keegan. His expression was as shocked as I felt.

"Does this mean we're not going to get punished?" Keegan asked.

Both my father and the chief burst into laughter.

"Oh, you're going to get punished," my father said. "Believe me, you're going to get punished!"

"Worse than you ever have in your entire life, no question," the chief said. "You're both going to regret this day for a long, long time."

"Part of being responsible for your actions is accepting the consequences," my father said. "Actions come with—"

There was a loud knock on the door, and before anybody could react it opened, and Mrs. Wallace popped her head in.

"You better come out and see this," she said.

"Whatever it is will have to wait," my father said.

"I don't think it can. We're next up on CNN."

chapter eleven

We all rushed out the door, practically bumping into each other. Mrs. Wallace turned up the volume.

"And this just in," one of the announcers said. "It's footage shot by a local cable company of a riot at a fall fair."

"Yes, and while it was your traditional fall fair," the female announcer said. "It was not your traditional riot."

The two announcers disappeared and were replaced by video of the parade coming down the street—everything looking normal.

"The Tomato Festival has been an annual event in Leamington for the last thirty-five years and, as the name would suggest, is a celebration of the tomato," said a voice-over of the male announcer.

"But during today's parade they found a new way to celebrate tomatoes!" the woman said.

The scene changed to a full-out tomato assault. They showed tomatoes flying through the air and smashing into members of the band, the peewee baseball team joining in, and then spectators adding to the melee.

"It continued for over ten minutes," the male announcer said.

There were more and more shots as the riot rippled up and down the parade route.

"It even hit the local beauty pageant contestants," the woman said.

"There's Kelsey!" Keegan exclaimed.

A barrage of tomatoes hit her and the two other girls in her car. Two of them ducked, but Kelsey jumped out of the car, ran over, grabbed some tomatoes from the wagon and began returning fire. She hit a guy right in the head as he was cocking his arm back to throw a tomato himself.

"I think we have the winner of the talent portion of the contest!" the female announced exclaimed.

Another camera angle came on the screen. There in the middle of it all was my father. He was the target for a number of tomatoes. It was awful to watch as he got hit repeatedly. Then he picked up a tomato himself and tossed it—hitting Mr. Miller squarely in the back!

We all looked at my father. He looked embarrassed.

"I was hoping nobody would see that," he said.

The two announcers came back on the screen.

"Reports are that there were neither arrests nor injuries," the woman said.

"To see more video of this event, or to find out more about Leamington and their Tomato Festival, please visit our website."

"We're the laughingstock of the country," my father said, holding his head in his hands.

"Isn't CNN broadcast internationally?" Keegan asked.

Was he trying to make things worse?

"Laughingstock of the entire world," my father groaned.

"I don't know about you," the male announcer said, "but that looked like a whole lot of fun, didn't it?"

"It did. It reminded me of the world-famous La Tomatina Festival," the woman said.

"The what?" I asked.

"The world's largest tomato festival held in Buñol, Spain," she said, like she was answering my question.

"Buñol features a daylong tomato fight, closing down a street to allow people to throw tomatoes at *anybody* along that section."

"It's sort of like the running of the bulls, involving tomatoes," the other announcer added.

"And today, Leamington put itself on the world map," she said, "challenging Spain as the biggest tomato celebration in the world."

"Leamington certainly staked its claim to be the most exciting festival in *our* county," he continued, "I know where *I'm* going next fall."

"Be sure to bring along a raincoat," she added. "Now turning to the latest developments in that earthquake that hit the coast of—"

Mrs. Wallace muted the TV, and we all stood there in silence, staring at the silent set.

"World famous," my father said.

"CNN coverage," the chief added. "Do you know how much coverage like that is worth?"

"You know," my father said. "I really wouldn't want to close off a section of street, but I wonder about the parking lot at the arena."

The chief nodded. "That would work. It's completely fenced on three sides, close enough to the other attractions, but contained and certainly far enough away from the parade route."

"You mean, you want to have a tomato fight?" I gasped.

"Well, of course," my father said. "Weren't you listening to the news at all? This could be an incredible opportunity."

"We were looking for something extra to add to the festival," the chief said.

"We could have people come from across the country. This could sell out hotel rooms, bring in more people to eat in the restaurants and shop at the stores. This could be amazing!"

"Does this mean we're not in trouble?" Keegan asked.

"Oh, no, you two are still in big trouble," my father said.

"Big trouble," the chief agreed.

"And as a big part of your punishment you both are assigned to the committee to arrange next year's tomato fight."

"I think we can do that," I said. "Now, if it's okay, do you think we could go and change into something not covered by tomatoes?"

"That would be wise," my father said.

"Yeah, I was hoping to catch the Miss Tomato Festival contest," Keegan added.

"That's a great idea," I agreed.

We strolled out of the office, leaving our fathers behind. We hurried down the stairs and out onto the street. The firemen were washing the last of the tomato skins and pulp into the sewers.

"Here, I have something for you," Keegan said. He reached into the front pocket of his stained jeans and pulled out a very squished tomato. "I was thinking that maybe it would be smarter if you carried it. No telling if I might see Owen and his tuba."

Eric Walters is the popular author of dozens of books for juveniles and young adults, including *Laggan Lard Butts* in the Orca Currents series and *House Party* and *Juice* in the Orca Soundings series. Eric lives in Mississauga, Ontario.